The
Bonsai
Beginners Guide

Oscar Jonker - Bonsai Empire

ISBN-13: 978-1981264155
ISBN-10: 1981264159

1. INTRODUCTION

Introduction to Bonsai

Bonsai trees are small, potted trees that are well-known parts of the Japanese culture. The living art of Bonsai represents peace and tranquility, as well as long-lasting determination and patience.

A "bon" is a flat tray or shallow pot, and "sai" means plant or planting. Originally from China, Bonsai trees date back hundreds of years and are well known for their miniature appearance. Bonsai trees can come in an array of types and can be grown in a variety of ways. They require daily grooming, but aren't high maintenance.

In this book, you'll learn more about the art of Bonsai and the history behind it, as well as tips for caring for your own Bonsai tree.

2. DESIGN PRINCIPLES AND INSPIRATION

Introduction to Design Principles

The ultimate goal of growing a Bonsai is to create a miniaturized but realistic representation of nature in the form of a tree. Bonsai are not genetically dwarfed plants, in fact, any tree species can be used to grow one. The best Bonsai – whether a single tree or a multi-plant or rock landscape composition – touch us, make us take notice, stop us as they catch our experience and imaginations to show us something new.

Thick trunks, textured bark, an interplay of twisting live wood and deadwood, surface roots, fine branch and twig ramification, foliage pads, relatively small leaves or needles, a complementary and relatively shallow container, tiny fruit or cones or flowers – these are just a few of the features that can be used to help portray a miniature landscape. They are not all needed or possible in any one given composition, and they cannot simply be included "just because". A true master artisan knows, feels what is needed. And his or her creation touches us, also. Those true masterpieces are the ones which, when you first look at them, can momentarily take your breath away and raise a smile.

Bonsai-in-training (also known as "potensai", potential Bonsai) should point to a future, more mature creation, in which the artist has somewhat in mind. And because these are made with living, growing things, those future pieces are never complete or finished. They will be presented within certain biological parameters, subject to health issues or remodeling by the tree with the caretakers' assistance.

The oldest and longest-containerized Bonsai because of natural changes can undergo several different styles throughout their long lives. These trees can, in fact, live longer than their full-size counterparts because of our increased attention to their health, water and nutritional needs, protection from weather extremes, injuries needing care, or pest infestations requiring containment or removal.

Techniques such as pinching buds, pruning and wiring branches, and carefully restricting but not abandoning fertilizers are used to limit and redirect healthy growth. Most commonly kept under four feet (or about a meter) in height, Bonsai are not genetically dwarfed plants. However, plants with smaller leaves do make these compositions easier to design. In fact, any plant species that has a woody stem or trunk, grows true branches, can be successfully grown in a container to restrict its roots/food storage capability, and has smaller or reducible-leaves can be used to create a Bonsai.

Look around at your trees, bushes, hedges, the copses in your yard or park, plants in the nursery or wild landscape – essentially any of those can be starter material.

Carefully collected during the appropriate growing or dormant season with proper permission, your composition is begun. Most native plants can be grown outdoors; material from more tropical climates needs at least some protection from the elements in the temperate zones.

Bonsai Size Classification

The ultimate goal of Bonsai is to create a realistic depiction of nature. As a Bonsai gets smaller (even down to a few inches/centimeters) it increasingly becomes abstract, as opposed to resembling nature in a more precise way.

Several classifications of Bonsai have been put forward, and although the exact size classifications are disputed, they help to gain understanding of the aesthetic and botanical aspects of Bonsai. The classifications are originally based on the number of men needed to lift the actual tree.

Keshitubo
1-3" (3-8cm)

Shito
2-4" (5-10cm)

Mame
2-6" (5-15cm)

Shohin
5-8" (13-20cm)

Komano
6-10" (15-25cm)

Katade-mochi
10-18" (25-46cm)

Chumono / Chiu
16-36" (41-91cm)

Omono / Dai
30-48" (76-122cm)

Hachi-uye
40-60" (102-152 cm)

Imperial
60-80" (152-203 cm)

Related arts

While "Bonsai" specifically refers to dwarf potted trees based on the Japanese model, it is also used as a generic term for related art forms in other countries, which include but are not limited to the following:

Penjing are the older and original form of Chinese miniature landscapes. They usually include rocks to represent mountains, hills, and cliffs. Sometimes they are even all the way up to 10' (or 3 meter) tall.

Saikei are the newer and smaller Japanese versions of penjing. These are made with rocks, small plants/groundcovers, and underdeveloped trees (which could someday become independently potted Bonsai).

Hòn non bộ are Vietnamese miniature landscapes from 1' to 25' (0.3 to 7.6 m) high, made with rocks, plants and water imitating island scenery, mountains and surroundings.

Mai-dăt are the Thai compositions which are more angular and symbolic, somewhat likened to stylized dancers' poses.

3. THE HISTORY OF BONSAI

Introduction to Bonsai History

Although the word 'Bonsai' is Japanese, the art it describes originated in the Chinese empire. By the year 700 AD the Chinese had started the art of 'pun-sai' using special techniques to grow dwarf trees in containers. Much later, the Japanese took over the art and refined it to what we know today as Bonsai.

China

From about the year 706 AD comes the tomb paintings for Crown Prince Zhang Huai, which included depictions of two ladies offering miniature landscapes with small plants in shallow dishes. By this time these were the earliest written descriptions of these pun wan – tray playthings.

As the creation and care of these was already somewhat advanced, the maturation of the art had taken place (but its documentation has not yet been discovered by the west).

The earliest collected and then containerized trees are believed to have been peculiarly-shaped and twisted specimens from the wilds. These were "sacred" as opposed to "profane" because the trees could not be used for any practical, ordinary purposes such as lumber. Their grotesque forms were reminiscent of yoga-type postures which repeatedly bent-back on themselves, re-circulating vital fluids and said to be the cause of long-life.

Over the centuries, different regional styles would be developed throughout the large country with its many varied landscapes; earthenware and ceramic containers would replace the porcelain ones displayed on wooden stands; and attempts would be made to shape the trees with bamboo frameworks or brass wire or lead strips.

Many poets and writers each made at least one description of tree and/or mountainous miniature landscapes, and many painters included a dwarfed potted tree as a symbol of a cultivated man's lifestyle. After the 16th century these were called pun tsai or "tray planting." The term pun ching ("tray landscape," now called penjing) didn't actually come into usage until the 17th century.

Japan

During the Kamakura period, the period in which Japan adopted most of China's cultural trademarks, the art of growing trees in containers was introduced to Japan.

The Japanese developed Bonsai along certain lines due to the influence of Zen Buddhism and the fact that Japan is only 4% the size of Mainland China. The range of landscape forms was thus much more limited. Many well-known techniques, styles and tools were developed in Japan from Chinese originals.

It is believed that the first tray landscapes were brought from China to Japan at least twelve hundred years ago, as religious souvenirs. A thousand years ago, the first lengthy work of fiction in Japanese included this passage: "A [full-size] tree that is left growing in its natural state is a crude thing. It is only when it is kept close to human beings who fashion it with loving care that its shape and style acquire the ability to move one". The first graphic portrayals of these in Japan were not made until about eight hundred years ago.

All things Chinese fascinated the Japanese, and at some point the Chinese Chan Buddhism also was imported and became Zen Buddhism in Japan.

Finding beauty in severe austerity, Zen monks – with less landforms as a model - developed their tray landscapes along certain lines so that a single tree in a pot could represent the universe. The Japanese pots were generally deeper than those from the mainland, and the resulting gardening form was called hachi-no-ki, literally, the bowl's tree. A folktale from the late 1300s, about an impoverished samurai who sacrificed his last three dwarf potted trees to provide warmth for a traveling monk on a cold winter night, became a popular Noh theatre play, and images from the story would be depicted in a number of media forms, including woodblock prints, through the centuries.

Everyone from the military leader shoguns to ordinary peasant people grew some form of tree or azalea in a pot or abalone shell. By the late eighteenth century a show for traditional pine dwarf potted trees was begun to be held annually in the capital city of Kyoto. Connoisseurs from five provinces and the neighboring areas would bring one or two plants each to the show in order to submit them to the visitors for ranking or judging. The town of Takamatsu (home of Kinashi Bonsai village) was already growing fields of partly-shaped dwarf pines for a major source of income.

Around the year 1800, a group of scholars of the Chinese arts gathered near the city of Osaka to discuss recent styles in miniature trees. Their dwarf trees were renamed as "Bonsai" (the Japanese pronunciation of the Chinese term pun-tsai) in order to differentiate them from the ordinary hachi-no-ki, which many persons cared for. The bon or pen is shallower than the hachi bowl.

This shows that at least some growers had better success with the horticultural needs of dwarf potted trees in smaller containers. Bonsai was now seen as a matter of design, the craft approach replacing the religious/mythical approach of tradition.

Different sizes and styles were developed over the next century; catalogs and books about the trees, tools, and pots were published; some early formal shows were held.

Copper and iron wire replaced hemp fibers for shaping the trees. Containers mass-produced in China were made to Japanese specifications and the number of hobbyists grew.

Following the Great Kanto Earthquake which devastated the Tokyo area in 1923, a group of thirty families of professional growers resettled twenty miles away in Omiya and set up what would become the center of Japanese Bonsai culture; Omiya Bonsai village. In the 1930s as formal displays of Bonsai became recognized, an official annual show was allowed at Tokyo's Metropolitan Museum of Art.

The long recovery from the Pacific War saw Bonsai become mature and cultivated as an important native art. Apprenticeship programs, greater numbers of shows, books and magazines, and classes for foreigners spread the word.

The use of custom power tools matched with an intricate knowledge of plant physiology allowed a few masters to move from the craft approach to a truly artistic-designing phase of the art.

Recently, Bonsai – seen too often as just a tired pastime for the elderly – now even has a version becoming popular among the younger generation with easy-to-care-for mini-trees and landscapes, unwired and wilder-looking, using native plants.

In 1604, there was a description in Spanish of how Chinese immigrants in the tropical islands of the Philippines were growing small ficus trees onto hand-sized pieces of coral.

The West

Although known to a limited extent outside Asia for three centuries, only recently has Bonsai truly been spread outside its homelands.

The earliest-known English observation of dwarf potted trees (root-over-rock in a pan) in China/Macau was recorded in 1637. Japanese dwarf trees were in the Philadelphia Exposition in 1876, the Paris Expositions of 1878 and 1889, the Chicago Expo of 1893, the St. Louis World's Fair of 1904, the 1910 Japan-Britain Exhibition, and at the 1915 San Francisco Exposition.

The first European language book (French) entirely about Japanese dwarf trees was published in 1902, and the first in English in 1940.

Yoshimura and Halford's Miniature Trees and Landscapes was published in 1957.

It would become known as "Bible of Bonsai in the West," with Yuji Yoshimura being the direct link between Japanese classical Bonsai art and progressive Western approach which resulted in elegant, refined adaptation for the modern world.

John Naka from California extended this sharing by teaching in person and in print first in America, and then around the world further emphasizing the use of native material.

It was by this time that the West was being introduced to landscapes from Japan known as saikei and a resurgence from China as penjing. Compositions with more than a single type of tree became accepted and recognized as legitimate creations.

Over the years, slight innovations and improvements have been developed, primarily in the revered old Bonsai nurseries in Japan, and these have been brought over bit-by-bit to our countries by visiting teachers or returning traveler enthusiasts. Upon their return from Japan, teachers would immediately try out a new technique or two in front of students at previously scheduled workshops. The new Japanese techniques could then be disseminated further and this living art form continued to be developed. With the release of The Karate Kid movies interest in the Bonsai art/hobby was spread amongst teens as well.

4. BONSAI STYLES

Introduction to Bonsai Styles

Over the years many styles to classify Bonsai trees have been advanced, closely resembling circumstances in nature. These styles are open to personal interpretation and creativity, meaning that trees do not necessarily need to conform to any form. Still, the styles are important to gain a basic understanding of shapes and can serve as guidelines to successfully train miniature trees.

Broom Style Bonsai

Hokidachi

The broom style is suited for deciduous trees with extensive, fine branching. The trunk is straight and upright and does not continue to the top of the tree; it branches out in all directions at about 1/3 the height of the tree. The branches and leaves form a ball-shaped crown that is also a stunning sight during winter months.

Formal Upright Bonsai Style
Chokkan

The formal upright style is a very common form of Bonsai. This style often occurs in nature, especially when the tree is exposed to lots of light and does not face the problem of competing trees. For this style, tapering of the upright-growing trunk must be clearly visible. The trunk must therefore be thicker at the bottom and must grow increasingly thinner with the height.

Informal Upright Bonsai Style
Moyogi

The informal upright style is common in both nature and in the art of Bonsai. The trunk grows upright roughly in the shape of a letter 'S' and at every turn branching occurs. Tapering of the trunk must be clearly visible, with the base of the trunk thicker than the higher portion.

Slanting Bonsai Style

Shakkan

As a result of the wind blowing in one dominant direction or when a tree grows in the shadow and must bend toward the sun, the tree will lean in one direction. With Bonsai, the leaning style should grow at an angle of about 60 - 80 degrees relative to the ground.

The roots are well developed on one side to keep the tree standing. On the side toward which the tree is leaning, the roots are clearly not as well developed.

Cascade Bonsai Style

Kengai

A tree living in nature on a steep cliff can bend downward as a result of several factors, like snow or falling rocks. These factors cause the tree to grow downwards. With Bonsai it can be difficult to maintain a downward-growing tree because the direction of growth opposes the tree's natural tendency to grow upright. Cascade Bonsai are planted in tall pots. The tree should grow upright for a small stretch but then bend downward.

Semi Cascade Bonsai Style
Han-kengai

The semi-cascade style, just like the cascade style, is found in nature on cliffs and on the banks of rivers and lakes. The trunk grows upright for a small distance and then bends downwards/sidewards. Unlike the cascade style, the semi-cascade trunk will never grow below the bottom of the pot. The crown is usually above the rim of the pot.

Literati Bonsai Style
Bunjingi

In nature this style of tree is found in areas densely populated by many other trees and competition is so fierce that the tree can only survive by growing taller then all others around it. The trunk grows crookedly upward and is completely without branching because the sun only hits the top of the tree. To make sure that it looks even tougher, some branches are "Jinned" (without bark). When the bark has been removed from one side of the trunk, the trunk is referred to as a "Shari".
The idea is to demonstrate that the tree has to struggle to survive. These trees are often placed in small, round pots.

Windswept Bonsai Style
Fukinagashi

The windswept style also is a good example of trees that must struggle to survive. The branches as well as the trunk grow to one side as if the wind has been blowing the tree constantly in one direction. The branches grow out on all sides of the trunk but will all eventually be bent to one side.

Double Trunk Style Bonsai
Sokan

The double trunk style is common in nature, but is not actually that common in the art of Bonsai. Usually both trunks will grow out of one root system, but it is also possible that the smaller trunk grows out of the larger trunk just above the ground. The two trunks will vary in both thickness and length; the thicker and more developed trunk grows nearly upright, while the smaller trunk will grow out a bit slanted.

Multitrunk Bonsai Style
Kabudachi

In theory the multi trunk style is the same as the double trunk style, but with 3 or more trunks. All trunks grow out of a single root system, and it truly is one single tree. All the trunks form one crown of leaves, in which the thickest and most developed trunk forms the top.

Forest Bonsai Style
Yose-ue

The forest style looks a lot like the multi-trunk style, but the difference is that it is comprised of several trees rather than one tree with several trunks. The most developed trees are planted in the middle
of a large and shallow pot. The trees are planted not in a straight line but in a staggered pattern, because this way the forest will appear more realistic and natural.

Growing on a rock Bonsai style
Seki-joju

On rocky terrain, trees are forced to search for nutrient rich soil with their roots, which can often be found in cracks and holes. The roots are unprotected before they reach the ground so they must protect themselves from the sun: a special bark grows around them. With Bonsai the roots grow over a rock into the pot.

Growing in a rock Bonsai style
Ishisuki

In this style the roots of the tree are growing in the cracks and holes of the rock. This means that there is not much room for the roots to develop and absorb nutrients. Trees growing in rocks will never look really healthy, thus it should be visible that the tree has to struggle to survive.
It is important to fertilize and water often, because there is not much space available to store water and nutrients.

Raft Bonsai style

Ikadabuki

Sometimes a cracked tree can survive by pointing its branches upward. The old root system can provide the branches with enough nutrients to survive. After a while new roots will start growing, eventually taking over the function of the old root system. The old branches that now point into the air develop into trunks with multiple branchings.

5. SELECTING YOUR BONSAI

Specific care guidelines for Indoor Bonsai

A common misconception about Bonsai trees is that they should be kept indoors. In fact, most Bonsai trees should be placed outside, where they are exposed to the four seasons just like normal trees are. Only tropical and subtropical plants can survive in the indoor climate of your house; where temperatures are high and stable throughout the year.

Indoor Bonsai trees; a Ficus, Carmona and a Chinese elm.

Can I have a Bonsai tree indoor?

There are several trees that you can grow indoor, but by far the most common (and the easiest to care for) is the Ficus Bonsai. The Ficus is tolerant to low humidity and can withstand quite a lot; a good choice for beginners.

Other popular indoor Bonsai trees include the Crassula (Jade), the Carmona (Fukien Tea), the Schefflera Arboricola (Hawaiian Umbrella) and the Sageretia (Sweet Plum).

Why can't I keep temperate (non tropical) Bonsai trees indoor?

The most important reason, as stated above, is that temperate trees need a period of dormancy (in winter). In this period the yearly growth cycle ends, and the tree prepares for the next cycle which will start again in early spring. A tree becomes dormant when temperatures and light intensity gradually decrease over the course of several weeks, which wouldn't happen when you keep your trees indoors.

Indoor Bonsai tree care

Caring for an indoor Bonsai tree is different from that of normal potted house plants. The main reason is that Bonsai trees are planted in small pots and therefore have limited storage for nutrients and water. More important is that tropical trees are used to much light and high humidity; circumstances that are quite difficult to create indoors.

Specific care of indoor Bonsai species

Light

The main problem with keeping a tropical indoor Bonsai tree is that the intensity of light indoors is much lower than outside. Trees won't die immediately when light intensity is too low, but growth will decrease, eventually weakening the plant. Therefore, make sure to place your Bonsai at a bright spot, preferably directly in front of a window facing the south.

Even when you have a window facing the south, chances are that the intensity of light is still too low. Artificial lighting can help, for example by using fluorescent lighting (with radiating growth-friendly spectra) or light-emitting diode lighting about 10 hours a day.

Humidity

Another issue with keeping a tropical Bonsai tree indoors is that the tree needs a relatively high humidity, much higher than the indoor conditions of your house (especially when you use heating or air conditioning). You can increase humidity near your Bonsai tree by placing it on a humidity tray filled with water and by misting your tree a few times a day. What also helps is to circulate air from outside, by opening a window during the day.

Watering and fertilizing

The most important rule is: never water on a routine. Ignore the label attached to your Bonsai tree which states you need to water every 'x'days. Instead, monitor your tree and only water when needed. Please read the watering and fertilizing pages for more detailed information.

Temperature

Tropical tree species need relatively high temperatures throughout the year, similar to the standard room temperature of your living room. Subtropical Bonsai trees can withstand somewhat lower temperatures, and generally thrive when they enjoy a winter season with temperatures well below that of the standard room temperature.

To summarize, make sure to select the right tree species and take into account the specific care guidelines for indoor trees, and you will do just fine!

Specific care guidelines for Outdoor Bonsai

A common misconception about Bonsai trees is that they should be kept indoors. Most trees should be placed outside, exposed to the four seasons, with temperature changes and a relatively high humidity.

Selecting an Outdoor Bonsai tree

You have a garden or a balcony and can keep your Bonsai tree outside, so you want an outdoor tree. Which one? The most important thing to consider is which conditions you can offer the tree and which species can live under these conditions. If you choose a native tree this is always a good idea, but keep in mind that many frost-hardy species need frost protection when they are planted in shallow containers.

Your local climate

If you live in a region with subtropical or mediterranean climate, you can grow many species outside which cannot endure frost, but some species must be protected from the heat and intensive sunlight.

Regions with a temperate climate are good for many species, especially most of the nice imported Japanese species can be grown successfully. Subtropical and mediterranean trees can also be chosen if they can be protected from frost, in a greenhouse for example.

In a maritime climate with moist summers you might need very well-draining soil and some species which need full sunlight might not be perfectly happy.

In a continental climate with hot summers and cold winters you will have to provide semi-shade in the summer and good protection against frost if you don't want to be limited to a few very hardy native tree species.

Conditions specific to your balcony / garden

It is important to also consider the special conditions in your garden or on your balcony. If you have full sun all day you can choose from a lot of species, but you might need some shade nets for sensitive species, especially if the Bonsai trees stand in a paved place surrounded by walls.

A garden with grass, shrubs and hedges can make a big difference because the air humidity is much higher most of the time.

If you live in a region with constant winds your trees need more water but will not so easily be infected by pests and fungal diseases.

Should you have a very shady garden or a balcony facing north or east there are only very few options. You could try a yew or a false cypress but although they might survive they won't be perfectly happy. Maybe you can do something to get more sunlight into your garden (chop down some large trees or shorten tall hedges) or move somewhere else...

Outdoor Bonsai tree care

Caring for an outdoor Bonsai tree is different from that of normal potted plants. The main reason is that Bonsai trees are planted in small pots and therefore have limited storage for nutrients and water.

More important is that Bonsai trees from temperate climates need their period of winter dormancy, but most species need some protection from frost and strong winds during that time.

Specific care of outdoor Bonsai Species

Light

Most outdoor Bonsai trees need sunlight for at least a few hours a day. Their internodes and leaves will grow too large otherwise and they get prone to pests and diseases then. Most conifers should be placed in full sun for healthy growth.

Humidity

On hot days and in a paved place surrounded by walls the trees can suffer from low humidity. You can increase humidity near your Bonsai tree by placing it on a humidity tray filled with water and by misting your tree a few times a day. What also helps is to wet the shelves, floors and walls around the trees.

Watering and fertilizing

The most important rule is: never water on a routine. Monitor your tree and only water when needed. This can be once in three days or several times a day, depending on the weather, species and size. Please read the watering and fertilizing pages for more detailed information.

Temperature

Outdoor trees can endure high temperatures as well as very cold weather if they are cared for properly. It is important for most species to provide protection from strong frost in winter. In spring, when the new leaves emerge, take care that the trees are protected even from light night frost.

To summarize, make sure to select the right tree species and take into account the specific care guidelines for outdoor trees, and you will do just fine!

6. CARE GUIDES

Introduction to Bonsai care guide

In this guide we take a closer look into tree-species that are often used for growing Bonsai. We discuss the guidelines for the ten most popular tree species in detail. Each species has specific requirements for its cultivation, training and care, so identifying your tree is crucial to take proper care of it.

Ficus	Juniper	Maple
Chinese & Japanese Elm	Azalea	Carmona
Pines	Jade-tree	Olive

An "s-curved" Ficus Retusa

The Ficus (Retusa, Ginseng)

The ficus genus belongs to the family of mulberry plants (Moraceae) and is the most popular indoor tree species for beginners at Bonsai. There is differing information about the number of existing ficus species, there may be between 800 and 2000. They live on all continents in the tropical regions and are very suitable for being kept as indoor Bonsai.

There are hundreds of varieties of the Ficus, but the most popular one for Bonsai is the Ficus Retusa, which is often shaped in an s-curved trunk and has oval, dark green leaves. The Tigerbark, Willow leaf, Golden Gate and Taiwan varieties are quite similar to the Retusa. The Ficus Ginseng is another popular tree. It has a thick, pot-bellied trunk, similar to the Ginseng root.

Some figs can become very large trees with a crown circumference of more than 300 m (1000 ft). Typical for all fig Bonsai species is their milky latex sap, which will leak from wounds or cuts. The tropical figs are evergreen trees, small shrubs or even climbing plants.

Another Ficus Retusa Bonsai

Some of them can produce nice flowers, while most ficus species have hidden flowers in small receptacles from which the fruit grow. Only specialized pollinating fig wasps can pollinate those hidden flowers. The fruit can be yellow, green, red or purple-blue and are between a few millimeters to several centimeters, like the edible fruit of Ficus carica.

Most ficus Bonsai trees can produce aerial roots in their natural habitat, which are often presented in appealing Bonsai creations with many aerial root pillars or root over rock styles. To enable aerial root growth in our homes a humidity of nearly 100% must be achieved artificially. You can use a glass cover, fish tank or a construction with transparent sheets for this purpose. Aerial roots grow down vertically from the branches and when they reach the soil they develop into strong pillar-like trunks. In tropical climates a single tree can become a forest-like structure and cover an enormous expanse.

The leaves of most Bonsai ficus species have special pointed tips from which the rainwater drips off. The leaves can be of very different sizes, between 2 and 50 cm long (1 – 20 inches). The trunks have a smooth grey bark in most cases. There are a few species or varieties however with special bark patterns, like the ficus microcarpa „Tigerbark" for example. Ficus Ginseng Bonsai plants are poisonous for pets, it can be especially dangerous if they eat the leaves. The trees should be placed out of the pets' reach.

Specific Bonsai Care Guidelines For The Ficus

Position: The Ficus is an indoor Bonsai which cannot endure frost. It can be kept outside in summer, if temperatures are above 59F (15 degrees C) and it needs lots of light – full sun is ideal, in the house as well as outside if the tree is exposed to the ultraviolet radiation gradually or if it is defoliated before placing the tree outside. A very shady position is unfavorable. The temperature should be kept relatively constant. Figs can endure low humidity due to their thick, waxy leaves, but they prefer a higher humidity and need extremely high humidity to develop aerial roots.

Watering: The Ficus should be watered normally, which means it should be given water generously whenever the soil gets slightly dry. The Bonsai Ficus can tolerate occasional over- or under-watering. Soft water with room temperature is perfect. Daily misting to maintain humidity is advised, don't overdo this otherwise fungal problems can appear. The warmer the position of the fig during winter the more water it needs. If it overwinters at a cooler place it only needs to be kept slightly moist. Continue reading about watering Bonsai trees.

Fertilizing: Fertilize weekly or every two weeks during summer, every two to four weeks during winter (if the growth doesn't stop). Liquid fertilizer can be used as well as organic fertilizer pellets.

Pruning: Regular pruning is necessary to retain the tree's shape. Prune back to 2 leaves after 6-8 leaves have grown. Leaf pruning can be used to reduce leaf size, as some ficus Bonsai species normally grow large leaves. If a considerable thickening of the trunk is desired, the ficus can be left to grow freely for one or two years. The strong cuts that are necessary afterwards don't affect the ficus' health and new shoots will grow from old wood. Larger wounds should be covered with cut paste.

A Ficus Ginseng plant

 Wiring: Wiring of thin to medium-strong ficus branches is easy as they are very flexible. The wires should be checked regularly though, as they cut into the bark very quickly. Strong branches should be shaped with guy-wires because those can be left on the tree for a much longer period.

 Special training techniques: Ficus has the ability to fuse plant parts which touch each other with some pressure. So branches, roots or trunks can fuse together and form appealing structures. You can use this feature for example to tie a lot of young plants together and let them fuse to build one strong single trunk.

Fig trees also react very well to approach-grafting of branches and roots and to other grafting techniques. If the growing conditions are ideal, even aerial roots taken from one part of the tree can be grafted in a different position. For faster closing of large wounds young plants, shoots or aerial roots can be grafted across the wound. The grower can work on fig trees with nearly unlimited creativity, which increases the appeal of ficus as a Bonsai plant considerably.

 Repotting: Repot the tree during spring every other year, using a basic soil mixture. Ficus tolerates root-pruning very well.

Propagation: Cuttings can be planted at any time of the year, but highest success is with mid-summer growth. Air-layering will work best in spring (April – May). Growing ficus plants from seed in spring also works easily in most cases.

Acquisition: Ficus plants are available as cheap Bonsai or pot plants in nearly every home-store, building supplies store or nursery. Mass-produced cheap Bonsai in most cases bring a lot of problems with them, like ugly scars from rusty wire that bit into the bark, unattractive shapes, often poorly grafted branches in odd positions, bad soil and sometimes inappropriate pots without drainage holes.
Specialized Bonsai traders offer everything from young plants, pre-Bonsai and pre-styled ficus trees up to high-value Bonsai, in most cases well-tended and of good quality.

Pests / diseases: The fig species are quite resistant against pests. Depending on the location, especially in winter, a number of problems can occur anyway. Dry air and a lack of light weaken the Bonsai ficus and often result in leaf drop. In a poor condition like this, ficus Bonsai are sometimes infested with scale or spider mites.

Customary systemic insecticide sticks to put into the soil or insecticide / miticide sprays will work, but the weakened ficus' living conditions must also be improved. Plant lamps (shining 12 – 14 hours a day) and frequent misting of the leaves during the recovery can be helpful.

Juniper Bonsai (Juniperus)

The juniper is a genus of about 50 - 70 species within the cypress family. They are evergreen coniferous trees or shrubs, which are very popular for Bonsai purposes.

Juniper Bonsai trees sold at large stores, including Walmart and Home Depot, are often Japanese Garden Junipers, also called Green Mound Junipers (Juniperus procumbens nana). Other popular species are the Chinese juniper (Juniperus chinensis), the Japanese Shimpaku (Juniperus sargentii), the Japanese needle juniper (Juniperus rigida), two central European species: the savin (Juniperus sabina) and the common juniper (Juniperus communis), and three American species: the California Juniper (Juniperus californica), the Rocky mountain Juniper (Juniperus scopulorum) and the Sierra Juniper (Juniperus occidentalis).

The foliage colors range from dark blue-greens to light greens and the foliage can either be scale-like or needle-like. Scale junipers usually have needle-like foliage when they are young (called juvenile foliage), the typical scale-like foliage appears later.

After heavy pruning or bending, overwatering or other stress often juvenile foliage will grow again. It can last a few years until enough normal scale-like foliage has grown and all the needle-like foliage can be removed.

The berry-like cones are round or oval, depending on the species they measure between 3 mm and 2 cm and they need a year or two to ripen. The seeds are round or edged. The cones are often eaten by birds who spread the germinable seeds later with their droppings.

Junipers are very suitable for creating deadwood (jin and shari). This is due to the fact that live veins below a broken or for other reasons dying branch will dry out and die. This results in natural deadwood which is peeled, polished and bleached by climatic conditions and is very durable in case of the juniper. The triad of green foliage, reddish-brown or yellowish-brown bark and silvery white deadwood is very appealing.

Specific Bonsai Care Guidelines For The Juniper

 Position: Place the tree outside, year-round, on a bright spot with lots of sunlight. The Juniper cannot live indoors. During the winter protect the tree once temperatures drop below -10 degrees C (14F). Some species change their foliage color during frosty periods to a purplish brown which is connected with their frost protection mechanism. In spring they will turn green again.

 Watering: Be careful not to water too much, as the juniper roots don't like soil wetness. Before you water, the soil should dry well. Misting the tree can be done regularly, especially after the tree has been repotted because it benefits from air humidity. Continue reading about watering Bonsai trees.

Feeding: Use normal organic fertilizer pellets or balls every month during the growth season or a liquid fertilizer each week. If strong growth is desired some higher nitrogen levels can be applied in spring.

Pruning: To develop the foliage pads, long shoots which stick out of the silhouette can be pinched or cut at the base with sharp scissors throughout the growth season. Do not trim the juniper like a hedge because the removal of all growing tips will weaken the tree and the cut will turn the needles brown. When the foliage pads become too dense they must be thinned out with sharp scissors at the base. The Juniper Bonsai is generally a strong tree that also withstands aggressive pruning quite well. But it cannot bud again from bare tree parts, so take care that there is some foliage left on every branch you want to keep alive.

Repotting: Once every two years, very old trees at longer intervals, using a basic (or somewhat more draining) soil mixture. Don't prune the roots too aggressively

Propagation: Use seeds or cuttings.

Wiring: Junipers which are produced for Bonsai purposes are already wired quite heavily in most cases when they are still very young. Dramatically twisted shapes are very popular and correspond with the natural shapes that used to grow in the Japanese mountains in former times. Junipers can be strongly bent, if necessary wrapped with raffia or tape as a protection, but you must be careful with parts which possess deadwood. Those parts break easily. If they are large and old, you can split the deadwood off in order to bend the more flexible living parts. The foliage pads should be wired and fanned out after thinning when necessary, to let light and air get in. Otherwise the inner parts of the foliage pads will die. In addition to this, the danger of pest infestation is increased if the pads are too dense. From the aesthetic point of view we also want to achieve unobstructed structures and want to prevent the juniper from looking like broccoli.

 Acquisition: Many well-suited juniper species in different sizes are offered in most nurseries. You can often find good Bonsai raw material there. In gardens, concrete pots and on cemeteries on old graves that will be cleared there are often quite old junipers and if you are lucky the owner will allow you to dig one out for little money or a new plant. Specialized Bonsai traders offer everything from young plants, pre-Bonsai and pre-styled juniper trees up to high-value Bonsai, in various styles
and shapes.

 Pests / diseases: If junipers are well cared for and placed in an ideal position they are quite resistant against pests. It is important though not to let the foliage pads get too dense, because otherwise pests can settle in them more easily. During winter the junipers must be kept in a place with enough light and they must be checked for pests regularly because pests can even occur in winter. Junipers can sometimes get infested with spider mites, juniper scale, juniper aphids and juniper needle miners as well as juniper webworms for example. Customary insecticide / miticide sprays will help but you should also find the reason why the tree was prone to infestation.

A big problem are fungal rust diseases. The diverse juniper species and cultivars have a very different level susceptibility to rust fungus, there are also some which are regarded as resistant. As a rule of thumb, the blue-green junipers are more resistant than those with yellowish-green foliage. The Japanese junipers are also not infested very often. In the internet you can find files which list many juniper species and cultivars and their susceptibility / resistance level to rust fungus.

The rust fungus infests the junipers permanently and causes swellings from which hard, brown galls emerge. In spring, during rainy weather, the galls produce large, orange, gelatin-like tendrils, full of spores, which infest the leaves of pear trees (but there are also types of rust fungus which use hawthorn or crabapples as a second host instead of the pear).

The fungus causes orange spots on the pear leaves. In late summer brownish proliferations grow from the bottom-sides of the leaves which release spores that infest junipers again. While the pear trees in most cases are not fatally affected – they are newly infested each year again and they can even be treated successfully with a fungicide, an infested juniper normally cannot be cured.

The visibly infested branches die in most cases and the fungus can emerge on other tree parts. Removing the parts with the swellings and galls is no guarantee at all that the fungus will not reappear. Although some people have a different opinion, it is best to immediately burn up a rust-infested juniper or put it into the garbage instead of your compost heap.

Japanese Maple (Acer Palmatum)

The green Japanese Maple (Acer palmatum) is originally from Japan, China and Korea. It owes its botanical name to the hand-shaped leaves with in most cases five pointed lobes (palma is the Latin word for the palm of hand). The bark of younger trees is normally green or reddish and turns light grey or grayish brown with age.

The greenish yellow flowers stand in clusters, appear in May - June and develop into maple seeds shaped like little paired winged nuts which float to the ground like propellers when mature. There are countless cultivars of the Japanese Maple with manifold leave colors and shapes and diverse habits and sizes, which are very popular as ornamental shrubs. The young shoots in spring have yellowish, orange or even bright red leaves. The Japanese Maple is also well-known and popular for its very attractive yellow, orange and red autumn colors.

Specific Bonsai Care Guidelines For The Japanese Maple

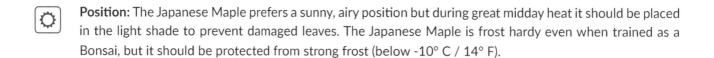

Position: The Japanese Maple prefers a sunny, airy position but during great midday heat it should be placed in the light shade to prevent damaged leaves. The Japanese Maple is frost hardy even when trained as a Bonsai, but it should be protected from strong frost (below -10° C / 14° F).

Watering: A Japanese Maple in a Bonsai pot must be watered daily in most cases during the growth season, maybe even several times a day during the hottest days, if the soil is well-drained and the tree healthy and vigorous. Use water deficient in lime as the Japanese Maple prefers a neutral or slightly acid pH-value.

Feeding: Especially for mature Japanese Maple Bonsai the use of solid organic fertilizers is well-proven, as it takes effect slowly and gently and generally contains all the required micronutrients. Follow the dosage instructions carefully. If stronger growth is desired, for example on young plants or raw material, you can additionally use a liquid fertilizer weekly. But avoid fertilizers with a very high nitrogen concentration because this would provoke unnecessarily large internodes and leaves.

Pruning: Trimming of shoots and twigs can be done year-round. The pruning of strong branches should be done in autumn to prevent excessive bleeding, or in the summer when callus growth is quick. It is advisable to apply cut-paste as the Japanese Maple is vulnerable to some fungal diseases which can enter through wounds. Cut new growth back to one or two pairs of leaves. Mature Bonsai with a delicate ramification can be pinched in order to keep the twigs thin.

After the first leaf pair has unfolded, remove the soft little tip of the shoot between them. This method weakens the tree in the long run and should be applied specifically and thoughtfully.

Leaf pruning (the removal of leaves during the growing season) can be done every other year in early summer to encourage smaller leaves.

Remove all the leaves, leaving the leaf-stems intact. Partial leaf pruning is more gentle. You do not remove all the leaves, but only the largest and closely spaced ones or you remove the leaves in the strongest areas of the tree. Partial leaf pruning can be done each year as it does not stress the tree as much as total leaf pruning.

Repotting: Repot Japanese Maple Bonsai once every two years and prune the roots efficiently. Root growth is strong and the pot is totally filled with roots after a short time. Use a well-drained soil mixture, for example Akadama mixed with a little humus and Kanuma.

 Pests and diseases: The Japanese Maple is quite a sturdy tree species. But in spring it is often affected by aphids, which can be eliminated with customary insecticide sprays and sticks to push into the soil. Verticillium wilt is a fungal disease which can provoke partial or total dying of the Japanese Maple. On fresh cuts you can see black spots in the wood. The disease is hardly treatable and other trees can be infected via the Bonsai tools. You should clean and disinfect your tools if Verticillium is suspected.

 Propagation: The Japanese maple can easily be propagated by seeds or cuttings in summer. Air-layering is also a quick and easy propagation method for Japanese Maples.

Chinese Elm (Ulmus Parviflora)

The Chinese Elm (Ulmus parvifolia) is endemic to south-east Asia and especially China. In its home countries it can become a mighty tree up to 25m tall and with 1 m trunk diameter. The Chinese Elm develops a fine ramification and small leaves very easily which makes it a very good Bonsai plant.

The Elm is often confused with the Zelkova but if you compare their leaves the difference is clearly recognizable. The Chinese Elm is the most popular Elm for Bonsai purposes although other elms are also very suitable.

Specific Bonsai Care Guidelines For The Chinese Elm

 Position: The Chinese elm grows well in full sun and also in partial shade. In mild climates it can stay outside during the winter. A Chinese Elm bought as an indoor Bonsai can be placed outside during the summer and in winter it is best to take it into a cold frost-free room. Chinese Elms can usually endure some frost but it seems that it differs depending on the region it was imported from. Trees from northern Chinese regions seem to be more frost-hardy that those from southern areas. Depending on the temperatures of their winter quarters Chinese Elms can either drop their leaves or keep them until spring when the new shoots emerge.

 Watering: The Chinese Elm must be watered generously as soon as the soil gets dry. Drought should be avoided as well as permanent wetness.

 Feeding: During the growing season the Chinese Elm should be fed well. It doesn't require very special fertilizer. A combination of solid organic fertilizer and a well-balanced liquid chemical product is a good concept. When the elm is in a cold place in winter it should not be fed during dormancy.

 Pruning: If you let the Chinese Elm grow freely it will thicken rapidly. It responds well to frequent trimming which produces a dense ramification and it also buds well from old wood after strong pruning. Allow shoots to extend to 3 or 4 nodes and then prune back to 1 or 2 leaves. A good time for pruning large branches of the Chinese elm is late autumn. The elm can be shaped very well with normal wiring and guy wires.

 Repotting: Younger Chinese Elms should be repotted every two years, older and large specimens can be repotted in longer intervals. Spring is the best time for repotting. Root pruning should be done with precision and as the Chinese Elm tends to produce crooked and intertwined roots you should work on them very carefully in order to create a regular nebari as good as possible. The Chinese Elm has no special requirements concerning the soil, but it should be well-drained. A standard soil mixture can be used.

 Propagation: Chinese Elm Bonsai trees can be propagated by cuttings without problems usually. Propagation by seeds is less recommendable.

 Pests and diseases: Often the Chinese Elm is infested by spider mites or scale when humidity is low. Appropriate pesticides should be used and frequent spraying with water might help additionally. Spraying with thinned lime-sulfur or systemic pesticides can make the Chinese Elm drop all its leaves, so avoid these products.

Zelkova (Japanese Elm)

This Zelkova, originally from Japan and China, is related to the Ulmus genus, which is the genus of the European and American elms. The Zelkova is in fact quite similar to the Ulmus (the Chinese elm), but it has single-toothed leaves whereas the Ulmus has double-toothed leaves. The Zelkova leaves are ovate, toothed and pointed.

Specific Bonsai Care Guidelines For The Japanese Elm

Position: Although an outdoor tree, when acclimatized to indoor conditions (often the case when bought in a garden center or so) it should be kept indoors at least during the winter. When placed outside however, protect the tree well during the winter. The tree prefers much light, not necessarily direct sunlight.

Watering: Water Japanese Elm Bonsai regularly.

Feeding: Fertilize the tree once or twice every month from spring till autumn.

Pruning: Allow shoots to extend at least 3 nodes then prune back to 1 or 2 leaves. Larger-leaved Zelkovas respond well to leaf cutting (defoliation) in summer.

Repotting: Repot the Zelkova Bonsai tree once every two years, less often when the tree matures, using a basic Bonsai soil mixture.

Propagation: Use seeds or cuttings.

Azalea (Rhododendron)

The Rhododendron genus contains about 1000 species, of which especially the Satsuki (Rhododendron indicum) and Kurume azalea (Rhododendron kiusianum and Rhododendron kaempferi) are commonly used for Bonsai.

The azalea is popular for its spectacular flowers, which open in May - June and come in many different colors, shapes, sizes and patterns. The leaves are dark green and differ in size and shape, depending on the cultivar. Satsuki and Kurume azaleas are evergreen, small shrubs which are very suitable for Bonsai purposes.

Specific Bonsai Care Guidelines For The Azalea

 Position: Azaleas thrive at a sunny spot, but during the hottest time it is better to provide some shade. When flowering, azaleas should be protected from rain and hot sun to make the flowers last longer. Healthy, mature azaleas can endure some frost but should be protected from colder temperatures than -5° C / 41° F.

Watering: Azalea Bonsai trees must not dry out but they also don't like permanent wetness. Because of this it is necessary to check the moisture of the soil very carefully. A root ball that has gotten too dry temporarily should be dunked in a bowl of water to get thoroughly moistened again. Azaleas need a slightly acid soil and hard tap water is not appropriate for them. You can use rainwater, mix rainwater with tap water or filter your tap water for the azalea Bonsai.

Feeding: During the growing season azalea Bonsai should be fed with a special azalea or rhododendron fertilizer. There are liquid azalea fertilizers which are used weekly and organic products to strew on the soil surface in longer intervals. While the trees flower quit feeding or use only half the normal dosage.

Pruning: The azalea is one of the very few tree-species that are basally-dominant. This means that the lower branches grow stronger than the weaker top, which leads to the shape of a shrub in nature. Therefore prune the branches at the base harder than the top. The Azalea withstands strong pruning very well and even produces new shoots from branches on which no leaves are left. Immediately after flowering the wilted flowers and ovaries are cut off or pinched by hand. This point of time is also favorable for all other pruning and trimming works because in summer the new flower buds for the next year will develop. If you prune your tree too late there will be no or nearly no flowers in the following year. Unwanted shoots from the trunk or the base of the branches can be removed at any time of the year. Extensive styling works on raw material are often done in spring and in that case flowering is omitted consciously. The wood of the azalea is brittle so that wiring and bending should be done with great care.

Repotting: Every two years, either in spring or after flowering, the azalea should be repotted. Prune the roots with great care because they are very thin and matted and can easily be torn when you try to disentangle them. It is important to use a special soil for azaleas which is lime-free. Pure Kanuma for example is a good azalea soil.

Propagation: Azaleas are propagated from cuttings in spring and summer. Depending on the cultivar the success rate can differ, but many customary cultivars produce roots easily and quickly. In the hot time of the year transparent sheets can be useful to protect the young cuttings from excessive evaporation.

 Pests and diseases: Azaleas are not often infested by pests. But low humidity can support spider mites which should be treated with a suitable pesticide and improved humidity. Vine weevil can eat the leaves and their grubs cause great damage on the roots. With special pesticides or nematodes the beetles and their grubs can be eliminated.

Root rot, caused by a fungus, can occur when the soil of the azalea is too wet and compacted. There are appropriate fungicides to pour into the soil that are effective against root rot. Another fungal disease causes leaf galls. In spring and summer leaves and possibly stems become thickened, curled, fleshy and turn pale green. In the later stages of the disease, the galls become covered with a white powdery substance and finally they turn brown and hard. Leaf galls are also stimulated by wetness and they appear most often on cultivars with plain-colored red and purple flowers. The best way to handle this disease is to remove the galls as soon as they are discovered and protect the azalea from too much rain.

Carmona (Fukien Tea)

The Fukien Tea is originally from China and it was named after the province Fukien, in Chinese Fuijan. It is also endemic in parts of Japan, Indonesia, Taiwan and Australia. The Fukien Tea is still very popular for Penjing in China and in Western countries it is a common indoor Bonsai tree.

Its small dark-green shiny leaves have tiny white dots on the upper side and are covered with hairs underneath. Small white flowers can appear all year round and sometimes produce small yellow-red to dark berries.

Specific Bonsai Care Guidelines for The Carmona

 Position: The Fukien Tea is an indoor Bonsai which can only be kept outside all year in very warm climates. It needs a lot of light and in the house it should be positioned behind a window pane where it gets the best light.

The perfect temperature is around 20 degrees C (68F), make sure it doesn't experience much lower temperatures. In summer the Carmona can be placed outside as long as the nights are warm enough.

In most cases the winter in our heated flats is a problem for the Fukien Tea. In addition to the few hours of daylight there is the problem of dry air. You can use a plant lamp if necessary and put a large tray filled with wet gravel or foamed clay under the pot for more humidity. When you open the windows in winter, take care that the Fukien Tea is not exposed to cold or even frosty air.

Watering: Keep the tree moist, as it doesn't like droughts. But be careful not to water too often because it doesn't like soil wetness either. As soon as the soil surface gets dry the tree needs to be watered generously but it must not be left standing in excess water.

 Feeding: Solid organic fertilizer is appropriate for the Fukien Tea Bonsai because its roots are sensitive. Liquid fertilizers can also be used in carefully measured dosage and only on moist soil. Feed the tree well from spring to autumn following the directions for use, but in winter less often.

 Pruning: The Fukien tree can take pruning quite well and regular trimming will make the tree grow a dense branch structure. Young shoots are tender and flexible so that they are easy to trim or wire. Mature twigs and branches are hard and brittle, so use appropriate tools for pruning and be careful when you want to wire and bend them.

 Repotting: Repot the Fukien Tea in early spring about every two years. Root pruning should be done with care because the Fukien Tea Bonsai does not take a great loss of roots well. A well-drained but on the other hand water buffering soil is very important because the Fukien Tea is sensitive to drought as well as excess wetness. A mixture of Akadama with a little humus and pumice is well-proven.

 Propagation: From seeds or by using cuttings in summer.

 Pests and diseases: Under inadequate conditions the Carmona Bonsai can suffer from spider mites, scale and whiteflies. Customary insecticide sprays and sticks to push into the soil will help but for long-term success also light and humidity must be improved. If the Fukien Tea is watered with hard water the leaves can show signs of chlorosis which can be treated with iron fertilizer. In rare cases fungal diseases can enter through wounds. They can kill single branches or even the whole tree and are hardly treatable. Use clean tools and treat fresh wounds with cut-paste.

Pine Bonsai (Pinus)

For Bonsai, pines are especially popular and many people even regard them as the most typical Bonsai trees. Pine trees are evergreen, coniferous resinous trees with needles that appear in bundles of two to five. The bark of older pine trees becomes scaly or flaky. Pines can grow in many different shapes in nature and can therefore be shaped in almost every known Bonsai style.

In order to treat each pine species according to its nature, it is necessary to know if it produces only one or two flushes of growth during the growing season. Pine species with two flushes can be decandled in early summer to produce a second flush with shorter candles and smaller needles. Pine species with only one flush of growth must not be decandled because that would harm them, but the candles can be selected and shortened. Check our website to identify your species of pine.

Specific Bonsai care guidelines for Pines

 Position: Place your pine outside in full sun. This supports healthy growth and helps decrease the needle size (needles grow longer if the tree doesn't get enough sunlight). Pine trees are very hardy, but still should be protected during the winter when they are planted in containers.

 Watering: Be careful not to over-water, as pines dislike permanent moisture. Good drainage is required. Protect the trees from excess rain while the shoots are developing because much water will make the needles grow longer than necessary.

 Fertilizing: Fertilize weak trees year round as long as the temperatures do not drop too low. Healthy trees are fertilized from early spring to late autumn.

 Pruning: Elongated candles should be shortened to an appropriate and even length from late spring to early summer. If there are more than two candles in the same place you can already cut off all but two. In autumn you can remove surplus shoots if you have not done so in spring. Read on our website about pruning two-flush pines.

 Wiring: Wire the pines from early autumn to early spring, or just after candles are shortened in early to mid summer.

 Repotting: It is best to repot in spring just after buds begin to move. You can also repot pines in late summer or early autumn when temperatures are not so high anymore but there is still enough time for the tree to regrow fine roots before winter.

 Propagation: Pines can be propagated from seed or grafting. Some can be air-layered and some can even be grown from cuttings.

 Pests and diseases: Pinus can be affected by aphids, spider mites, scale or caterpillars. Sometimes they are also attacked by fungal diseases and root rot. Specific pesticides must be used in that case and it is recommended to get help from an expert in that situation.

Dwarf Jade (Portulacaria afra)

Originally from Africa, the Jade tree is a fleshy, softly woody shrub or small tree up to 3m. The Jade has a thick trunk and a fine branch structure with thick oval green succulent leaves. During autumn sometimes small white flowers appear, but only when the tree has experienced droughts in the season. The bark is green and soft when young, becoming red-brown when it ages.

Specific Bonsai Care Guidelines For The Jade

 Position: The Jade tree is considered an indoor tree in most temperate zones, although it can be grown outdoors in full sun (and sufficiently high temperatures). Keep temperatures above 5 degrees C (or 41F) at all times. It needs lots of light or even full sun.

Watering: Jade trees can hold large amounts of water inside their leaves. Water sparsely and allow the plant to dry out a little bit between watering. During winter time watering can be as seldom as once every three weeks. The Jade Bonsai is not as particular about over-watering as most other succulents.

Feeding: Once a month during the growth season (spring-autumn).

Pruning: As a succulent, water is contained its trunk and branches; they tend to bend from their weight. Jades respond well to pruning, which should be done regularly to force the tree to grow branches also lower on its trunk. Do not use cut-paste though, as this might lead to rotting.

 Repotting: Repot the three every second year in spring, using a very well-draining soil mixture.

 Propagation: Easy to propagate using cuttings during the summer.

Example of a Dwarf Jade (Portulacaria afra)   *Example of a Jade (Crassula ovata)*

Olive (Olea europaea)

The olive (Olea europea) is a tree commonly found in Mediterranean countries, where it is a tree with strong symbolic importance. You can use cultivated varieties (like the normal olive) but it is common to use the wild olive (Olea europea silvestrys).

The wild olive is of greater interest for Bonsai as these develop tiny leaves. In many cases these possess much appreciated features like the presence of jin, shari and bark that indicate a high age and survival in hostile conditions. The Olive as Bonsai tree is easy to care for and very strong so it is a suitable choice for use as Bonsai.

Specific Bonsai Care Guidelines For The Olive

Position: Place the Olive Bonsai outside and at a sunny spot, this also helps to reduce the size of the leaves. Must be protected during the winter if temperatures get too low.

Watering: No specifics.

Feeding: Feed abundant, with a normal fertilizer monthly from spring to mid autumn.

Pruning: Strong pruning is recommended in late winter. The olive will respond with vigorous growth in the following spring. For maintenance pruning, cut back to 2-3 pairs of leaves, and in very vigorous (and healthy) specimens you can use defoliation.

Repotting: Repot in spring before the buds begin to swell, every three or four years. Preferably use a soil mix with good drainage.

Propagation: From seeds and cuttings.

7. TECHNIQUES

Introduction to Bonsai technique

Bonsai trees are normal plants, propagated like any other, but trained using sophisticated techniques to make and keep them miniaturized. The styling of Bonsai trees includes basic techniques like regular pruning and wiring, but also more advanced techniques such as creating deadwood.

Caring for a Bonsai tree is not as hard as is commonly thought. However, as Bonsai trees are planted in small pots a few basic guidelines have to be followed when watering, fertilizing and repotting your trees.

Watering Bonsai trees
How to water your trees

The most important part of taking care of your Bonsai trees is watering. How often a tree needs to be watered depends on several factors (like species of tree, size of tree, size of pot, time of year, soil-mixture and climate), indicating that it is impossible to say how often you should water Bonsai. However, understanding a few basic guidelines will help you to observe when a tree needs to be watered.

How often should I water?

As mentioned above, how often Bonsai trees need to be watered depends on too many factors to give exact guidelines. Instead, you need to learn to observe your trees and know when they need to be watered. The following general guidelines will help you to get Bonsai watering right:

- **Water your trees when the soil gets slightly dry**
  This means you should not water your tree when the soil is still wet but only when it feels slightly dry; use your fingers to check the soil at around 0.4" (one centimeter) deep. Once you get more experienced you will be able to see (instead of feel) when a tree needs watering.

- **Never water on a routine**
  Keep observing your trees individually, instead of watering them on a daily routine, until you know exactly what you are doing.

- **Use the right soil-mixture**
  The soil-mixture greatly influences how often trees need to be watered, for most Bonsai trees a mixture of akadama, pumice and lava rock mixed together in a ratio of ½ to ¼ to ¼ should be fine. However, use a mixture that retains more water (by using more akadama, or even potting compost) when you cannot water your trees that regularly.

When watering this tree, most water will flow right out of the pot; the roots are so compact that the soil-mass won't absorb water easily. This tree needs to be repotted!

When?

It doesn't really matter at what time you water a Bonsai. Some advice to avoid watering (with very cold water) during the afternoon, when the soil has been warmed up by the sun and will cool down rapidly when using cold water. Though this can be taken into consideration, it should always be clear that you should water your tree no matter what time it is, as soon as the soil gets slightly dry!

How to water Bonsai trees?

As explained previously, water when the soil gets slightly dry. When the tree does require water though, it needs thorough soaking so the entire root system is wetted. To do so, keep watering until water runs out of the drainage holes, and possibly repeat the process a few minutes later.

Water a tree from above using a watering can with a fine nozzle; this will prevent the soil from being washed away. Using collected rain water is better (as it doesn't contain added chemicals), but when this is not readily available there is no problem in using normal tap water. There are also automated watering systems, but these are often quite costly.

Fertilizing Bonsai
Feeding is crucial for Bonsai trees

Feeding regularly during the growth season is crucial for your Bonsai to survive. Normal trees are able to extend their root system looking for nutrients; Bonsai however are planted in rather small pots and need to be fertilized in order to replenish the soil's nutritional content.

Basic file parts of fertilizer

The three basic elements of any fertilizer are Nitrogen (N), Phosphorous (P) and Potassium (K), with each element serving different purposes. Nitrogen increases growth of leaves and stems (growth above ground), Phosphorus encourages healthy root growth and growth of fruits and flowers, Potassium promotes overall plant health. Different ratios of NPK are being used for different trees at different times of year, which is very important to take into account when fertilizing Bonsai.

When should I apply fertilizer?

Fertilize during the entire growth season of the tree; from early spring till mid autumn. Indoor trees can be fertilized around the year. Although sometimes disputed, do not fertilize repotted trees for about a month; also do not fertilize sick trees.

Biogold is an organic fertilizer from Japan, often used for Bonsai trees.

Which fertilizer to choose?

It is very important to choose the right fertilizer for your Bonsai plants: during the early spring time use a fertilizer with a relatively high Nitrogen content (something like NPK 10:6:6) to boost the tree's growth. During the summer use a more balanced fertilizer (like NPK 6:6:6) while during the autumn use a fertilizer to harden off the tree for the coming winter (like NPK 3:6:6). Instead of changing your fertilizer ratios throughout the year, you can also use the same fertilizer, but slowly reduce the quantity applied towards late fall.

A few exceptions are worth pointing out: to encourage Bonsai to flower use a fertilizer with a high Phosphorous (P) content (like NPK 6:10:6) and for older trees you might want to use fertilizer with a slightly lower Nitrogen (N) content or reduce the quantity of fertilizer applied.

Although "Bonsai fertilizer" is fertilizer like any other, buying from (online) Bonsai shops will help you find the right NPK values. Any fertilizer with the right NPK value is perfectly fine. You can choose to use either liquid or solid fertilizer; which doesn't matter much, just follow the application guidelines as stated on the product's packaging.

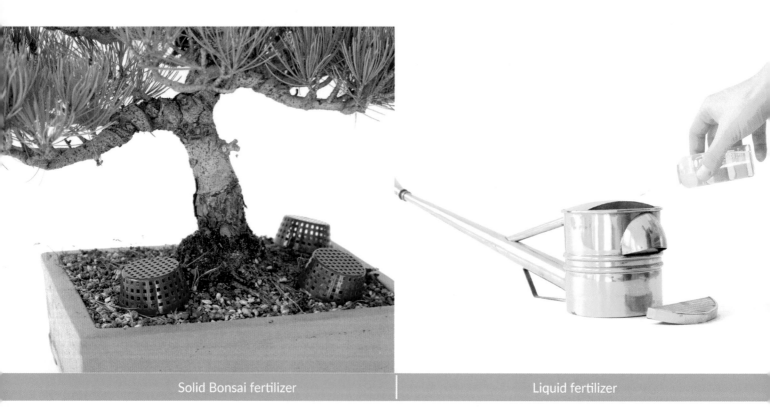

Solid Bonsai fertilizer | Liquid fertilizer

How to fertilize Bonsai trees?

Feed your Bonsai using the quantities and frequency as stated on the fertilizer's packaging. You can choose to reduce the recommended quantity slightly for trees that are not in training anymore, to balance their growth instead of stimulating it. When using solid fertilizer it helps to use fertilizer covers, which make sure the fertilizer stays in place. Never overfeed your trees, as this will have serious consequences for their health.

Fertilizing a Bonsai, step by step

1. The tree we want to fertilize.

2. When using a solid and organic fertilizer, we like Biogold, Aoki and Tamahi. But you can select other brands of course!

3. Put the fertilizer in cups / baskets, to make sure it is not washed away while watering or eaten by birds.

4. The cups are than placed onto the soil surface.

5. On this size of tree and pot, we place three baskets filled with Biogold fertilizer.

6. We can however also choose to feed the tree with a liquid fertilizer.

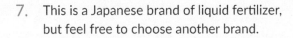

7. This is a Japanese brand of liquid fertilizer, but feel free to choose another brand.

8. Read the fertilizer instructions to learn how often and in which quantities to apply the Bonsai fertilizer.

9. The liquid fertilizer is applied while watering your tree.

Key take-away

Fertilizing your Bonsai is very important, as the soil mass is limited for most Bonsai trees. Overdoing it however, is a sure way to harm your tree!

☼ Positioning your trees
Placing your tree at the right spot

Deciding on what is the best location to place your Bonsai trees can be hard, as several factors (local climate, time of year, tree species, etc.) should be taken into consideration. Best is to know what species of tree you have and to look for specific information about it.

Bonsai position: rule of thumb

Most outdoor trees are best placed on a bright spot, about half the day in direct sunlight and protected from the wind.

Indoor trees are best placed on a bright position as well; some species prefer lots of sunlight while others prefer half shade. Place indoor trees somewhere with a constant temperature.

Indoor Bonsai trees; a ficus, carmona and Chinese elm.

Outdoor trees; a juniper, pine and maple.

Repotting Bonsai
How to repot your tree

To prevent a tree from being pot-bound and ultimately starving to death, regular repotting is crucial. Re-potting your Bonsai will not keep it small; instead it will supply the tree with new nutrients that it needs to grow and flourish.

How often should I repot?

It depends on the size of container/pot and tree species how often a Bonsai needs to be repotted. Fast growing trees need to be repotted every two years (sometimes even every year), while older, more mature trees need to be repotted every three to five years. Do not repot on a routine, instead check on your trees every early spring by carefully removing the tree from its pot. A Bonsai needs to be repotted when the roots circle around the root system. When the roots are still contained in soil wait another year before checking again.

This tree needs to be repotted as the roots circle around the root mass.

When?

Repotting work normally needs to be done during the early spring; when the tree is still in dormancy. This way the somewhat damaging effect of repotting on a tree is reduced to a minimum, as the tree does not yet have to sustain a full-grown foliage. Repotting in early spring will also ensure that damage done to the root system will be repaired soon, as soon as the tree starts growing.

Bonsai soil mixture

Choosing the right soil mixture is crucial for the health of your trees, it should be draining enough to prevent the roots from rotting, while absorbing enough water to supply the tree with water. Although some tree species need special soil mixtures, the following mixture is suitable for most trees:

Mix Akadama, pumice and lava rock together in a ratio of 2:1:1. When you do not have time to water your trees regularly, choose a more water absorbing mixture (use more Akadama), while you should choose a more draining mixture (use more lava rock) when living in a wet climate.

"Choosing the right soil mixture is crucial for the health of your trees."

Choice of Bonsai pot
Choosing a pot that fits your Bonsai, both in size as in style, is crucial for the composition.

Repotting Bonsai, step by step

1. Make sure you have the right tools to repot your tree; a rootrake, scissors, wire cutter and a chopstick.

2. Often Bonsai are anchored to the pot they are planted in; in that case cut the wire.

3. Remove the tree carefully from its pot, using a rootrake.

4. We can now evaluate if repotting is necessary; in this case it is, as the roots are circling around the inside of the pot.

5. Using a chopstick we start removing the old soil, starting on the sides and bottom of the tree. Try to avoid damaging roots in the process. When repotting pines, leave at least half the rootmass untouched to protect the mycorrhizal fungus which is essential for the tree's survival.

6. Using scissors, cut away any roots that have grown too long. Do not prune more than 30% of all roots.

7. In this case we repot the tree into the same pot. We prepare the pot by covering the drainage holes with mesh.

8. The mesh are held in place with a piece of wire.

9. We also attach an additional wire, which we will use to stabilize and anchor the tree to the pot later.

10. Add a thin layer of heavy grain soil first, like lava rock, grit or akadama, which serves as a drainage layer.

11. Next add another thin layer of Bonsai soil.

12. Place the tree in its pot. We use the wires attached earlier to hold the tree in position.

13. Add Bonsai soil around the tree.

14. Use your chopstick to work the soil around the roots, making sure to fill all the air pockets around the root system.

15. Finally, we water the tree thoroughly.

16. This is what the tree looked like two weeks after repotting.

Key take-away

The most important thing to keep in mind is timing. Repot your tree right before the growth season starts; in early spring.

Pruning Bonsai
Cutting branches to shape your tree

Without doubt the most important way to train a Bonsai is to prune it on a regular basis. Essentially, there are two different techniques: maintenance-pruning, to maintain and refine the existing shape of a Bonsai - and structural-pruning, which involves more rigorous pruning to give a tree its basic shape or style.

Before discussing both techniques in more detail it is useful to look at some background information on how trees grow. This will help us understand how to prune Bonsai trees most efficiently.

Trees have a natural tendency to distribute growth to the top (and to a lesser extent outer parts of branches) which is called 'apical dominance'. This natural mechanism encourages trees to grow higher in order to prevent them from being shaded out by competing trees. By distributing growth to the top and outer edges the tree's inner and lower branches will eventually die, while top branches grow out of proportion; two effects not desirable for the design of Bonsai trees. This basic background reveals the importance of pruning as a technique to counter apical dominance. Countering apical dominance is achieved by pruning the top and outer portions of a tree more thoroughly, forcing the tree to redistribute growth to the inner and lower parts.

Part 1: Bonsai maintenance pruning

The goal of maintenance pruning is to maintain and refine the shape of a tree. As explained above, trees will concentrate most growth on the top and outer parts of the tree; it is important to prune these growth areas regularly in order to encourage growth closer to the inner parts of the tree.

When to prune Bonsai?

Maintenance pruning can be done throughout the growth season, usually March to September.

How?

As mentioned previously, maintenance pruning is required to maintain a trees' shape. To do so, simply prune branches/shoots that have outgrown the intended canopy-size/shape using twig shears or a normal cutter. Using the right Bonsai tools will help significantly.

Don't be afraid to prune your Bonsai; it is important, especially in the outer and top areas, to prune regularly in order to force the tree to distribute growth more evenly and develop a dense foliage. As opposed to deciduous trees, pine trees and some conifers should be pinched by hand. Using scissors to prune some species of conifers would lead to dead brown foliage at the cuttings.

To prevent this from happening hold the tip of the shoot between your thumb and pointing finger and carefully pull it away; the shoot will snap at its weakest point and no brown ends will appear. Different species need different maintenance regarding pruning and pinching; some even need a combination of both. Please consult our species guides for information per tree species.

Pruning a pine (incorrect)

Pinching by hand (correct)

Another method of Bonsai pruning is defoliation, which involves removing leaves of deciduous trees during the summer to force the tree to grow new leaves. This technique ultimately leads to a reduction in leaf size and an increase in ramification.

Part 2: Structural Bonsai pruning

To give a tree its basic shape often involves pruning large branches. Deciding on which branches should stay and which ones should be removed can be difficult, not only because it is an irreversible action but also because it is part of deciding how the tree will look like. Before learning more about the techniques used for pruning Bonsai, you might want to take a look at the Bonsai progressions part of the Bonsai Empire's website, where you will find examples of experienced Bonsai growers structure-pruning nursery stock.

When?

Overall, the early spring and in some cases late autumn is the right time to structure-prune a tree (just before and after the growth season). In the tree species section you can check the specifics on your particular tree, a Ficus Bonsai needs different timing from a Juniper Bonsai for example.

How?

Place the tree on a table at eye-level; first step is to remove all the dead wood from the tree. Now take some time to observe your tree and decide which branches do not fit the desired design and will need to be removed. A few guidelines are listed below, but deciding on the future design of your tree is a creative process, not necessarily bound by 'rules'.

A Few Basic Guidelines:

- If two branches occur at the same height of the tree, keep one of them and remove the other.

- Remove vertical growing branches, which are too thick to bend.

- Remove branches with unnatural twists and turns.

- Remove branches that conceal the front of the trunk.

- Remove disproportionately thick branches from the top of the tree, as branches at the bottom should be thicker than at the top.

Pruning thick branches will result in creating ugly scars on the tree, but by using a special concave cutter you will reduce this effect significantly because of the indentation it makes when cutting off the branch.

A healthy tree should have no problem coping with pruning up to 1/3 of the trees foliage. Some theories prescribe to cut/remove an equal percentage of roots after a tree has been styled. Most experts however agree on performing only one big maintenance per time (or even once a year). This would mean that you structure-prune this spring and wait with repotting until the next spring (when the tree has fully recovered from the structure-pruning). More details about pruning roots can be found at the root flare (Nebari) page.

Finally, it is advisable to seal large cuttings with wound paste, available at most (online) Bonsai shops. The paste protects the wounds against infections and helps the tree to heal faster. Again, using the right Bonsai tools will help significantly.

1. Suckers that grow from the base of the trunk
2. Branches blocking view on the trunk
3. Limbs that grow close to the ground
4. Hanging branches
5. Dead branches
6. Crossing branches
7. Branches returning to the center of the tree
8. Upward growing interior branches
9. Branches with unnatural twists and turns
10. Parallel growing branches
11. Suckers higher on the trunk (water sprouts)
12. Branches extending beyond the tree profile
13. Branches growing from the same height on trunk
14. Branches that compete with the trunkline
15. Disproportionately thick branches at the top

Grey branches are considered 'errors' and can be removed. Ultimately, pruning is not about following strict rules, but about establishing the best design for your tree. This illustration only serves to provide some general guidelines.

Pruning Bonsai trees, step by step

1. This Ficus needs to be pruned, as several long shoots have grown out of shape.

2. Using a Twig shear we prune long shoots.

3. In this case, we removed about 20% of all leaves.

4. Pruned material

5. When pruning larger branches, we use a concave cutter. On this photo you see the shape of the cutter; which leaves a hollow wound which will heal faster than flat wounds.

6. Create some space to make the cut, by first pruning the majority of the branch.

7. By removing the majority of the branch, we now have space to make a clean cut exactly where we want it.

8. We cover the hollow wound with wound paste, which will help the tree heal the wound quicker.

9. We use a Japanese brand of woundpaste, but you can select any brand you like.

10. The wound covered with woundpaste.

Key take-away

Maintenance pruning can be done year round, postpone structural pruning until the next spring however.

Wiring Bonsai trees
Bending and shaping the branches of a Bonsai

Wiring is a crucial technique to train and style Bonsai trees. By wrapping wire around the branches of a tree you are able to bend and reposition the branches. It will take a few months before the branches are set in their new shape; the wire should than be removed.

When?
Wiring can be done year-round for most tree-species. Most deciduous species should be wired in late winter, the absence of leaves makes wiring much easier. During the growth season branches grow thick quite fast and as a result the wire will cut into the bark, creating ugly scars. Check on your tree regularly and remove the wire on time.

Material?
Using the right material is essential for wiring Bonsai trees. Basically, two kinds of wire can be used: anodized aluminum and annealed copper. The aluminum wire is used for deciduous species, while the harder copper wire is used for conifers and pines. For beginners it is advisable to use the anodized aluminum wire, which is easier to work with and sold in most (online)
Bonsai shops. Wire is available in a range of different thicknesses, varying from 1 to 8 mm. There is no need to purchase all the available wires; buying 1mm, 1.5mm, 2.5mm and 4mm thick wire should be perfect to start out with. When wiring thick branches it is recommended to wrap them first with raffia, which will protect the branches from being damaged by the wire when bending them.

Copper wire | Aluminum wire

How to wire a Bonsai tree?

Wiring is a tricky technique to master. Try to wire two branches of similar thickness located near each other with one piece of wire (double-wiring) where possible, and wire the remaining branches separately (single-wiring). Wire all the branches you intend to shape before actually bending them. When wiring an entire tree, work from the trunk to the primary branches and then start wiring the secondary branches. As a rule of thumb, use wire of 1/3 of the thickness of the branch you are wiring. The wire should be thick enough to hold the branch in its new shape.

Both wiring techniques will be discussed in more detail now and information about how to safely bend the wired branches will be provided at the end of this page. A step by step guide follows below. Using the right wire and Bonsai tools will help significantly.

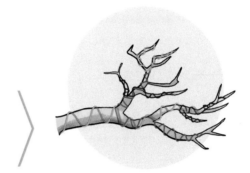

We try to wire two branches with one piece of wire, with as little wires crossing each other as possible. This illustration only serves to provide some general guidelines, each tree is different.

Part 1: Double wiring a Bonsai

- First select the pair of branches you will wire; these have to be of the same thickness and located near each other on the tree. Do keep in mind that the wire should wrap around the trunk at least once (preferably twice) so the wire will not move when bending the branches later on.

- Now cut off the right length of wire to wrap around both the branches.

- Start with wrapping the wire around the trunk and proceed with the first branch. Wire from the base of the branch to the very tip before starting to wire the other branch. The wire should be wrapped around the branches at an angle of 45 degrees; this way the wire will enable the tree to grow thicker while remaining its new shape.

- When you intend to bend a branch downwards directly at the trunk make sure the wire comes from below. The wire should come from above when bending a branch upwards.

- After you have wired all suitable pairs of branches continue wiring the remaining branches using the single-wiring technique.

Part 2: Bonsai branch single wiring

- Similar to the double-wiring technique, cut off the right length of wire and start with wrapping it at least twice around the trunk at an angle of 45 degrees.

- When multiple wires are applied at the same part of the trunk/branch try to put them neatly in line.

- Now continue wiring the branch.

Bending the wired branches

After having wired the entire tree you can start bending and repositioning the branches. Use your hands to hold the outside of the branch with your fingers, now bend the branch from the inside of the curve with your thumbs. This way you reduce the risk of splitting branches by spreading the force around the outside of the branch. When a branch is in position stop moving it, as repeated bending will likely damage the branch. Try to bend straight sections of branches slightly to make it look more natural.

And then? Aftercare

Place the tree in the shade and fertilize as you would normally do. Watch the tree closely during the growth season and remove the wires in time to prevent them from cutting into the bark. Do not try to recycle wire by unwinding it as this might damage the tree; instead, cut the wire at every turn making it much easier to remove.

Wiring Bonsai trees, step by step

1. This is the branch we will wire.

2. Selecting the proper thickness of wire can be tricky at first. In this case we selected a 3mm thickness. Wrap the wire around the branch in a 45° angle.

3. Using a wire cutter we cut the wire.

4. This side branch is then wired with a 2mm wire. We first wrap the wire neatly in line with the previously applied 3mm wire, before wrapping it around the side branch.

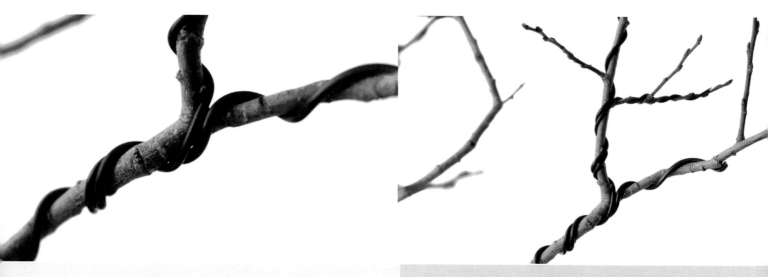

5. Closeup view.

6. From the side branch, we wire the smaller branch growing to the right with a 1mm wire.

7. Once completely wired, we bend the branch and its side branches into position and shape.

8. The lowest branch on the left of this Bonsai tree needs to come down a bit. We will use a guy-wire to bring it down.

9. First we wrap some protective material around the branch and then we apply a 'hook' with a thick piece of wire.

10. The guy-wire can be attached to the Bonsai pot, or like in this case, to a strong root.

11. Using a thin wire we connect the branch with the root, and carefully bend the branch downwards until we are satisfied.

12. Be very careful to check on your tree when it is wired; you want to remove the wires before they grow into the branches. These scars look ugly and artificial.

Key take-away
Wiring is a tricky technique to master. Practice and you will get better at it!

8. START NOW

How to grow your own Bonsai

Buying a Bonsai tree in a shop is nice, but wouldn't it be much better to do it yourself? A great way to start growing Bonsai trees is to buy a starterkit and style the tree into a Bonsai. A Bonsai starterkit usually contains a young plant (called a pre-Bonsai or a nursery stock), a Bonsai pot, wire and soil.

A starterkit can be purchased at many (online) Bonsai shops, but you could also choose to buy only a young plant at a local garden center. On our website you will find a location finder to Bonsai stores near you.

This article explains the steps to create a Bonsai tree from a starterkit. It shows parts of our online course "Getting Started with Bonsai", where we teach the steps to create a Bonsai tree.

The complete course is priced $10, but one lecture is free and shows the pruning, wiring and repotting of a nice Juniper plant. See: www.youtube.com/watch?v=L1FDfwyjkrs

Step 1: Pruning your Bonsai tree

First of all, we start to clean out the tree. Carefully study your tree, and decide on what shape you intend to create in it. While it is easy to prune branches, it can be very hard to make them grow back. Once you have decided which branches should be removed, prune these, slowly working your way up the tree. Start with freeing up the trunk a bit.

When pruning larger branches, you need a concave cutter. This cutter leaves behind a hollow wound, which heals much better. After pruning the larger branches, focus on smaller branches, until you are satisfied with the result.

Step 2: Wiring your Bonsai

Next, we wire the branches, starting with the larger ones. Carefully apply wire around the branches at an angle of about 45 degrees. Try to wire two branches of the same thickness with one wire. As a rule of thumb, apply wire about 1/3 the thickness of the branch.

When you're done wiring the larger branches, work your way towards the smaller ones. Finish wiring the entire tree, before you start positioning and bending the branches.

Step 3: Placing your tree in a Bonsai pot

Now that we have pruned and wired the tree, it is time to repot it.

To get started, we prepare the Bonsai pot. Place two wires that can be used later on to attach the tree firmly to the pot. We also cover the watering holes by attaching a plastic mesh.

When the pot is ready, we prepare the soil mix. Usually a starter kit comes with premixed Bonsai soil, but if not, check our website for more information.

Now remove the plant from its plastic container and get rid of any loose soil. We also want to reveal the trunk a bit. Carefully unravel the roots using a root-hook.

To make the tree fit in the pot, you will need to prune away roots. You can prune up to about 1/3 of the total root mass. Now, put some soil in the pot.

The tree is now ready to be placed in the pot, but first, decide on what the front of the tree should be. Place the tree just off the center and attach it carefully with the wires that were attached in the pot earlier.

Cover the roots with soil and by using chopsticks we make sure that the entire rootmass is filled with soil. When we're done, we water the tree.

That's it!

Now we have a Bonsai tree; pruned, wired and repotted. So what's next? Remove the wire after a few months, otherwise the branches would get damaged as they grow thicker. Place the tree in the shade the first month after repotting.

In this article we used a Juniper, worth around $20, but starterkits can contain any kind of tree species. Make sure you know what tree species you have, and look up its specific care guidelines in our Bonsai tree species section.

9. CONCLUDING REMARKS

Conclusion

This guide is our attempt to help beginners appreciate and learn about the living art of Bonsai. It wouldn't have been possible without the support of several Bonsai experts and friends of Bonsai Empire. There were many, but specifically we'd like to thank Bjorn Bjorholm, the Luis Vallejo Bonsai collection (photographer Miguel Krause) and Robert Baran.

To continue your learning experience, we highly recommend to take a look at some of the online courses we have created. The curricula and some free lectures can be found here: **www.bonsaiempire.com/courses**

Made in the USA
Monee, IL
29 May 2021